Himalayan Adventures

By
Penny Reeve

Christian Focus Publications

For Richard with love,
for Binod and friends with hope,
and for Jesus my Lord,
the author and perfector of my faith.

Contents

Where my Help Comes from

It was breakfast. I was just cutting into my second pancake when Shirley and Helen pushed the dining room door open, their faces red and their hair damp with sweat. "They don't exist!" said Helen as she slumped in the nearest chair and began tugging off her hiking boots. "I tell you, they do not exist!"

"What are you two talking about?" I asked, confused. "Where have you been? You almost missed breakfast."

"Oh, we better not have!" said Shirley. "If there are no mountains, and no pancakes either, what on earth are we doing here!?"

"No mountains? This is Nepal, of course there are mountains," I said.

"Not today," said Helen. "Today they do not exist."

"Or at least, if they do, they didn't want to be seen by us." Shirley dumped her bag on one of the lounge chairs and walked across to the table.

Shirley and Helen had just walked back from Sarangkot hill, the best look-out site in Pokhara. They had woken up while it was still dark, climbed the hill and waited for the sun to paint the mountains as it rose for the day.

"There was nothing up there," Shirley explained as she helped herself to the syrup. "It was such a shame. We got there nice and early, before the buses of tourists had arrived and crowded everything, but even from the look-out tower we could see nothing. It was all cloudy, even then, we couldn't see a thing!" She poured herself a cup of tea and sat back with a sigh.

I looked out the window to where I knew the mountains were, but there was just whiteness. These days the clouds race to cover the mountain peaks, and if it isn't cloudy it is smoggy and the mountains bare ghosts somewhere in the distance. There are days, however, when the sky is clear and the Himalayas loom over us as if they grew out of Pokhara's backyard.

"Oh, well," I said trying to be encouraging, "you can go again another time... ."

Helen and Shirley exchanged looks and laughed. "Yeah, but not for a while!" They were exhausted.

The Nepalis say that "Nepal's riches are found in nature" and every year the Himalayas draw visitors to Nepal from all over the world. Germans, Israelis, people from the UK, Korea, India, America, they all come to see the mountains and most of them do. They take off on treks, some guided, some independent and then they leave taking memories and photos of this amazing place with them. But there are some people who come to Nepal who don't leave so quickly. They have the chance, even if they don't feel like it immediately, to climb Sarangkot again, and again and again. They are people like Helen and Shirley, and us, who have come to Nepal to work for a while.

Working and living in a country other than your own can be an adventure. An adventure in which you take God's hand and follow where he leads you. But it can also be hard work. You have to say goodbye to the places and people you love and come somewhere totally foreign. There is the language to learn, and that takes months and years. There are weird customs to get used to, some that you like (drinking lots of tea) some that you don't (religious rituals that wake you in the middle of the night). It can be difficult to make friends, to know how to stay healthy and not continually get sick with diarrhoea (we've had our share of that!). Sometimes, as life gets hard, it is easy to forget who it is you are serving and why you ever started on the adventure anyway.

I remember one time, when we were in language school and everything seemed impossible. We were struggling over verbs and vocabulary and adjusting to the oppressive monsoon climate when one of our friends reminded us to look up.

"We keep looking down," he said one morning.

"We jump over puddles and cow poo and open drains. We have to dodge the taxis and the kids racing in and out of school. You can get so busy looking at the ground and looking where you are going, that you forget to look up and see the mountains. Look up! See Machhapuchhare.... it is just standing there, even if we can't see it everyday because of the rain or weather, but it is there, pointing upwards and reminding us of God."

The Nepalis say that Machhapuchhare is a sacred mountain. They say that no one has ever or will ever climb it because it is so sacred anyone who tries will die. Before the climbing of this mountain became prohibited there was one team, in 1957, that attempted to reach the top. This

expedition got to 50 meters of the summit before the Nepali climbers refused to go up any higher. They were afraid of the anger of the gods if they were to climb the holy mountain. But we know that the mountain is not sacred. It is part of creation, made by the Holy One. To us it can be a reminder that God is in control and that even if we can't see him - if we are looking all the time at our problems, or life just seems foggy, he is still there. He is loving us always. Watching us always. Caring always. We just need to lift our eyes up and focus on Him.

I lift up my eyes to the hills, where does my help come from?

My help comes from the LORD, the Maker of heaven and earth. Psalm 121:1 and 2

The Bat and the Yershi Tree

Nepal is quite a small country, it is shaped like a sausage with the northern border hidden in the Himalayas and the southern border running along vast flat plains. In between the plains and the mountains are the valleys and hills and it is in this area of Nepal, in the lower foothills of the Himalayas, 1000 metres above sea level, that the Chepang people live.

The Chepang people are one of Nepal's many ethnic

groups. They have their own language and many unique customs. Unlike other people groups who like to build their villages in clusters and groups, the Chepang people scatter the homes in their villages along the ridges of hills. If they look up they can see the mountains that make Nepal famous. If they look down they can see the Terai and India. All around them are deep gorges and steep rivers and the jungle in which the tree the Chepang call Yershi grows.

The Yershi is a very big tree with large leaves. The branches spread out like a canopy leaving the underneath bare, cool and shaded. In winter the tree flowers and at the end of the branches clusters of small creamy yellow flowers appear which are full of sweet nectar. When the flowers fall off the tree they have a hollow centre through which you can thread a stick or a string. After the flowers come the nuts which can be ground and steamed and eaten which is probably why another name for the tree is Indian Butternut. But, if you take one Yershi tree, and a pitch black night, you could go hunting with the Chepang.

The Chepang are expert bat hunters. In the middle of a winter night they get up and take their nets. Then, following the jungle paths they have memorized, they find a Yershi tree laden with flowers. If I was to go with them I am sure I would trip and fall down some steep hillside, but they know their jungle so well they can travel this way even in the dark. Once they reach the tree they set up their nets strung open wide between a bamboo pole and the tree. One end of the net is secured firmly to the ground and tree, the other is attached to the pole held by a hunter further away. Once the invisible wall of netting is installed under the tree's canopy the hunters then wait. Perfectly still and perfectly quiet they sit,

hoping that when the bats do arrive their squealing will not attract leopards.

Some bats in the Himalayan region eat fruit, others eat insects and bugs and still others eat nectar. It is the nectar eating bats which come to feed from the flowers in the Yershi tree. They suck out the sweet nectar as their main source of food, not realizing that tonight they will be caught and become food themselves. As the bats fly under the tree they fly straight into the Chepang nets. The person holding the pole then swings it around, closing the net and trapping the bat between the folds of net. Then the bat is pulled down, the net opened again, and another bat caught. Sometimes, on a good night, the Chepang hunters can catch up to 20 bats under one tree. And that means a great meal.

While I was hearing about the way the Chepang people hunt bats under the Yershi tree, I couldn't help thinking about the Creator of our world. He didn't just make things here and there and hope that, by chance, they would all work together nicely. No, the Yershi tree makes beautiful nectar, the nectar attracts the bats who in turn fertilize the tree while they eat. The tree is nice and tall with an easy canopy underneath, perfect for hoisting up a net. And the Chepang catch some of the bats to supplement their diet with added protein. Isn't it great that when we trust God, we are trusting a God who has a plan and a purpose for everything? He knows what we need to grow and live. He knows what makes Yershi trees flower and why bats like the sweet nectar - because that is how He created the world. Nothing was an accident. Everything in creation has His signature on it. Even Yershi trees and nectar-eating bats and people like you and me.

In the beginning God created the heavens and the earth. God saw all that he had made, and it was very good. Genesis 1:1 and 31

Eagle's Eyes

Adokho is a large cone shaped basket woven out of strips of split bamboo. The weave is wide and makes large round holes so you can easily see what is inside the basket. If you place a loop of rope around the basket and up onto your head you can carry the dokho securely on your back. I have seen these baskets used for many things. My friend Karuna, who is ten years old, places large plastic containers in her dokho and carries water from the public tap to her house each morning. Her father has an even bigger one which he fills with cow manure and carries down to the corn fields at the bottom of the hill. These baskets are used for collecting animal fodder, for selling cauliflower, or mandarins, or green bitter spinach the Nepalis call saag. But I would say the most interesting use is when the basket is emptied and turned upside down, sometimes with a rock or old sack on top. It is when the dokho is on the ground like this that it starts cheeping!

The basket itself doesn't cheep, of course, it is what is underneath that starts making the noise. In the rural houses of Nepal, dokhos are used as temporary hen pens. They are especially useful for protecting a hen who has a brood of chickens. In Nepal the household chickens have quite a few predators. They might get snatched away at night by a roaming leopard. They might be dragged off into the bushes by a nauri-musa (a sort of Nepali mongoose). Or, while happily pecking and scuffing in the yard they might be spotted by an eagle.

Eagles in Nepal, like anywhere else, have terrific eyesight. They fly up extremely high and soar on the gusts of rising air, all the time keeping an eye focused on the ground. Up there they are too high for the hens and chickens to notice them. In fact, most of the time they go unnoticed by everyone, even people. They can silently, secretly pick out their next meal from the mother hen's brood and then fold their wings inwards and pummel downwards, squealing as they come.

The squeal from the eagle alerts not only the owners of the chickens, who start waving their arms around wildly and shouting "hha! hha! hha!" to scare the eagle away, but it also warns the mother hen. Carefully she starts clucking a specific type of cluck and her little chickens freeze solid still. This amazing trick seems to totally confuse the eagle. He can no longer see the frightened chicks huddling quietly close to the ground. All he sees are the angry owners of the chickens throwing up threats and stones. So, reluctantly he has to give up this attack and fly away. He might hover again and wait for the chickens to scurry about again, or for the owners to sit down and drink tea, or he might try another household. But as soon as the mother hen realizes the eagle has gone, and danger has passed for now, she clucks again. This time it is a different cluck which means "OK, it's safe now, lets find some more grain" and the chickens all begin scratching around again... either that or their owners hurry them under a dokho for the rest of the afternoon.

Those chickens know the clucking of their mother so well that even among the confusion and fear of an eagle attack they can follow her directions. I wonder if we listen that carefully to what our Father in Heaven has to say to us? There is a verse in the Bible that says *"I will hasten and not delay to obey your commands."* Psalm *119:60.* God's word is worth listening to. It is full of instructions and help for us. There are stories there that can encourage us to keep going. There are words that help us know what to think in confusing times, words that reassure us of God's unfailing love, and words that warn us about what can hurt us. Obeying God can sometimes be scary, but when we remember that he is our creator, and that he knows what is best for us, we can know that listening to him and obeying his commands is guaranteed to be the safest thing we could ever do.

Your commands make me wiser than my enemies.

Psalm 119:98

Morna's Monkey

Our house is only five minutes walk from our daughter Lillian's school, but even in this short distance there are a lot of animals. There are usually at least three cows on the football field, including one very big bull who seems to think the world belongs to him. There are chickens and ducks on the road and a goat in someone's shed. Someone else owns homing pigeons, and across the road from that house is a buffalo kept for milk. Sometimes we see all these animals in the one trip to school, sometimes we only see Jack the three-legged dog that belongs to my friend Morna, but one day I saw something unusual for our part of town, there was a small tan-coloured monkey tied up in a tree.

What made it unusual was not the fact that it was a monkey, there are lots of monkeys in Nepal. Many Himalayan people even believe there is a 'monkey god'. The huge temple areas of Kathmandu swarm with monkeys on the weekends, racing after people carrying bags of peanuts or pieces of fruit. No, seeing a monkey wasn't unusual, but the fact that it was sitting in a tree in our part of Pokhara was.

The little monkey, who we later discovered had been named Kanchi by her earlier owners, had round loop earrings in her ears and a charm around her neck. She was quite a handful right from the start. Morna had once told me about an unhealthy little monkey she had seen sitting on the shoulder of a local Hindu priest. She had felt so sorry for the monkey that she had promised herself that if she ever saw another one tied up and mistreated like that, she would rescue it. And now there was a monkey sitting on her front fence.

Morna knows quite a lot about animals. She is a vet. She was the one who cut Jack's broken and sore leg off. She knows what to do if a puppy swallows chicken bones, she has operated on cows and cats and at one stage owned eight dogs. But I must admit, I did wonder how she would cope with a monkey, what she would do with it, how she would feed it?

The first problem was obviously to find the monkey a cage because although Kanchi was a wild animal it would need some restriction if it was going to stay near people. Keeping it locked up inside the house wouldn't work because not only was Kanchi not toilet trained, she was quite mischievous. After only half an hour of being locked in Morna's son's room she had made a total mess. Morna found the little critter sitting on the

floor on top of one of the wall posters it had pulled down, chewing the blue-tack like chewing gum! They needed to get a cage. So Morna removed the monkey's jewellery and took her to a local carpenter. There she ordered a nice large cage as quickly as they could make it so that Kanchi could spend part of her day tied by a long string climbing trees and part of it in her new cage. But, even with routines like that, Morna knew that Kanchi was still not a pet.

Kanchi was a wild animal. She was only about six months old when Morna first got her, still young enough to be feeding from her mother's milk. She was supposed to be in a troop of other monkeys, with her sisters and aunties. Although Morna let the little Rhesus monkey sit on top of the doorway and watch the family eat breakfast, or sit on the windowsills to watch the children play, Kanchi was still a monkey.

In those early monkey days, Morna spent quite a bit of time researching information about the Rhesus monkey. In the wild this type of monkey feeds on fruit, insects and seeds. Normally they will live to about four years old, but in captivity (like in a good zoo or a similar enclosure) they can live for up to thirty years! A female monkey, like Kanchi was likely to grow to about ten kilograms. One of the interesting things that Morna told me she had learnt was that Rhesus monkeys have a tendency to think they are superior to people.

These monkeys will choose someone to be affectionate with (probably a female), choose someone else to obey (most likely a male) and then decide they are better than everyone else. At Morna's house it went like this: Kanchi loved Morna like her own mummy.

She respected Morna's husband, Brad, and would be well behaved for him, but she didn't like the children. She was bossy and nasty and looking for a fight. Morna had to be very careful where the monkey was tied up in relation to the kids, but no matter how often she tried to warn the monkey or train it, Kanchi still thought she was boss.

Sometimes people are just like Kanchi. They boss other people around because they think they are in control. They like to be better than others, and even if they don't say it all the time, they probably really think they are. But God doesn't want us to be full of pride. Jesus said that we are to love one another. It is hard to really love someone when you keep thinking about how much better you are! Love, the Bible says, is not proud (1 Corinthians 13:4) and love is what keeps us from being monkeys.

For by the grace given me I say to every one of you: Do not think of yourself more highly than you ought. Romans 12:3

Do you want to know what happened to Kanchi? With Morna's help she found herself a new home, one where she could be safe, well fed, and among other monkeys. And maybe one day she will turn thirty!

Yeti or Not?

Have you heard of the Yeti? It is big and hairy, dark, fierce and wild. It lives up, above the snow line, walking upright on the look out for food. It comes when it wants. Leaves when it wants and all it ever leaves behind are enormous footprints. The Yeti is listed as one of Nepal's endangered animals. You can take a mountain flight on Yeti Airlines and stay in the 'Yak and Yeti' hotel. You can buy a handmade 'Yeti doll'

in the tourist district of town. But no one can actually prove it exists.

When I decided to research this mysterious creature I borrowed some books from a local library and read up what I could. I didn't have the resources to set out on an expedition but some people have done that. They pack months of supplies and camp in some distant valley. Then they go out day after day with researchers and trackers, following legends and footprints, always hoping to catch a glimpse of this elusive animal.

Expeditions have searched the Himalayas but Yeti footprints seem to be the only evidence found. These footprints were larger than human footprints, but very human-like in appearance. The feature that identified them as possible Yeti prints was the thumb-like big toe, not unlike the foot of a monkey. Human feet do not have this characteristic. Estimates made from measuring and studying these prints show a likely weight for the creature of around 70 kilos. It walked upright and some people have even claimed to have seen it in the distance raising its hand above its eyes as it looked around.

One girl said that she had seen the Yeti up close. She described it as having a wrinkled forehead with shrunken eyes and a body covered in hair. She saw this creature on the same day that five yaks were killed by something that twisted their heads off by the horns! But no one from the village had attempted to kill the yaks. It makes you think, doesn't it? You begin to wonder if maybe there is a savage yak killing beast in the Himalayas... .

But, people who are familiar with snow, tell me that a footprint in the snow will grow. As the sun comes and heats up the ice, and the wind blows across the print it can get bigger. A normal human size foot print can appear larger than normal, and out of proportion,

like that of a Yeti perhaps? And as for the eye witness accounts of the Yeti... have you been outside when it is snowing? The falling snow blurs your vision, especially if it is falling thick and fast. How do we know that those who claim to have seen the Yeti were not gazing through a snow storm? Or what about after the snow has fallen fresh and pure and the sun rises and glares down making a blinding field of white? How can you see clearly on days like that? Or maybe they were hallucinating, seeing things as a result of mountain sickness, having climbed up too high too fast?

Maybe the Yeti was just a Himalayan bear? Both the Himalayan Black Bear, easily recognized by the fantastic V-shaped white marking on its chest, and the Brown Snow Bear venture high up into the mountains. They can both stand and walk upright for periods of time, some people have even seen them raise their paw to shield their eyes from the glaring sunlight. And, although they feed mainly on plant matter like berries and fruit, they can attack large animals. The Brown Bear has been known to attack goats and ponies. The Himalayan Bear can be very dangerous to people if it is alarmed in its own territory.

Brown Bear? Yeti? Hallucinations? I suppose we will just have to keep wondering about the Yeti. It could be there... or maybe it is just a legend. Like the Loch Ness Monster of Scotland, or the Big Foot from North America, it continues to keep us guessing. Fortunately our God is not like that. Some people will say to you "Prove it!". They will quote weird and strange situations and confusing statements to show how we cannot really know that God is there. But there is a verse in the Bible that challenges us to *"Taste and see that the Lord is good."* *Psalm 34:8.* How do you know if something is good or not if you don't taste it? How will you ever find anything if you don't really ever start looking?

We can know for sure that God is real. He has communicated his existence to us in creation, he has communicated his love for us in the Bible. We can see him acting in people's lives, in the miracles we hear about or even see. He has promised us that if we are looking for him, if we are looking with all our heart, we will find him.

"I will be found by you," declares the LORD. *Jeremiah 29:14*

I like that verse. Yeti or not, our God is there and we can find him!

Bear Escape

Ram had just returned from working in the millet fields. He wasn't very happy. The fields had been pretty badly damaged by a local bear. "We've got to do something about this bear," he grumbled.

"Won't he just go away by himself?" one of the younger boys asked.

"No. Now he knows where the easy food is, he'll just keep coming back. The only way to stop him will be to kill him. Otherwise he might get dangerous," said Ram. He started preparing his hunting tools.

"Can I come too?" Ross asked from where he was sitting with some neighbours chatting. "I've never been bear hunting before," he added. Ram nodded slightly and continued to get ready. Ross walked over to tell Kathleen where he was going. "You be careful," she said as the men started walking off into the jungle.

Ram and Ross walked away from the village, into the jungle, until they came across a bear trail. It was a well used track that the bear had used recently. There were fresh footprints on the track and Ram guessed that the bear would come back this way sometime soon, probably on its way to the millet fields again! Ram measured the footprint carefully.

"What are you doing?" asked Ross.

"You can see how tall the bear is by the size of the footprint," Ram explained. "You multiply the size of the footprint by 2.5 and that tells you how high the bear is."

Ross was impressed and continued to watch as Ram began setting up the trap. It was the type of trap that relied on an exact measurement of the bear's height. As the bear came past the trap it would trigger the release of a spear which would pierce the bear in the heart region. If the measurement was correct the spear would hit its mark perfectly. After Ram had finished preparing the trap he and Ross went back to the village, talking eagerly of how they would divide up the meat among their friends. Tomorrow they would return to the trap and recover the bear.

But the next day, when Ross and Ram came back to check the trap they found that the trap had sprung, but there was no dead bear waiting for them to carry home. Ram rubbed his forehead confused, then bent down to study the tracks. Ross bent down too, but all he could see were flattened leaves and scuff marks. "What happened?" he asked.

"The bear came... ," said Ram studying the ground, "but he was coming down hill from the village, not going up to the fields like we had expected."

"What does that mean?" asked Ross, feeling very unlearned.

"We set the trap to shoot the bear coming up, it shot him...," Ram picked up the spear, "see, it has blood on the arrow tip, and some fur, but the bear didn't die. Look at the bushes... "

Ross looked down the hill where Ram was pointing.

"They have all been flattened, but in a messy way, not like bears usually move. That bear has been wounded and is very angry." The two men squatted on the ground a bit longer and then Ram stood up. "We will have to get some of the others," he said and he started walking back up to the village. Ross walked behind him and thought about the bears that lived in this region of Nepal. He knew that the Himalayan Bear roamed these hills, as did the Sloth Bear. The Himalayan Bear can be quite dangerous. It has been known to attack people if it is startled or if its young are nearby, but they can also attack for no apparent reason. Ross had also heard of one man who was chased by a Sloth Bear until he climbed a tree to escape, and even then the man had had to beat the bear off with his sickle to survive. Ross wasn't sure he wanted to meet a bear up close, Sloth or Himalayan, especially one that had been wounded by a trap he had helped set.

Eventually Ram had gathered a few of the other men from the village. Some of them were carrying bows and there was an atmosphere of adventure. The women stood in their doorways shaking their heads. "You'll be killed," one of them called out. The men discussed the situation a bit more and then set out to follow the wounded bear. Once they reached the trap they became quiet. Several men whispered about the more correct height of the bear, others just kept their eyes on the trail of flattened vegetation. They were looking for further signs of distress but there were none. The bear must have been shot, perhaps in the shoulder, enough to make it angry but not enough to slow it down. It had raged away down the hill until it reached a dark and narrow gully.

Some of the men went into the gully after the bear. Ross and a few others decided it would be safer to climb to the top of the gully to watch from above. If the bear was really in there it would have no way to escape, it would be trapped, the men coming from one end and the gully closing off at the other. Ross waited up the top listening, but he couldn't hear or see anything. Time dragged on and there was still nothing. Eventually, after imagining what an angry bear could do to the villagers and expecting the worse, he saw the hunters emerge from the jungle. They were tired, but there were no signs of a battle.

"What happened?" Ross asked Ram on the way back to the village.

"It had gone away." said Ram. "I don't know where, we lost its tracks in the gully. But we couldn't find it... ," he paused, "and I think maybe it was a good thing that we didn't. Let's just hope it doesn't come back this way anytime soon."

That story makes me think: if the gully was as it was described to me, and the bear prints led into it... then surely it was inevitable that the men would find the bear, sore and raging... but they didn't. I wonder if it was a miracle, if God prevented them from finding the bear, knowing it would seriously hurt some, if not all, of them. God's grace is like that. We get ourselves in a lot of messes. We do things we shouldn't, say things we shouldn't but even when we know we have done wrong, God's grace is big enough to cope with that situation. We can never mess up too much for his forgiveness to handle. Not only can he forgive us but he can help us fix up the situation we have fumbled.

But he said to me, "My grace is sufficient for you, for my power is made perfect in weakness." 2 Corinthians 12:9

Mountain Ambulance

S hanti-maya was sick. Her husband, Sri, had watched day after day as she had become thinner and thinner. He didn't know what was wrong with her, neither did anyone else, but somehow without anyone telling him, Sri knew his wife was going to die.

He was almost desperate when he called in the local Jhakri. This was the village 'holy' man, the man who worked magic and supposedly told the evil spirits what to do. Medicine hadn't cured Shanti-maya, maybe the Jhakri could. But after several weeks, and quite a bit of money being paid out, Shanti-maya called for her husband to come and talk to her. There were tears running down her cheeks as she told him to marry again after she died. "You need someone to be a mother to our children," she explained, but Sri didn't want to listen. He didn't want his wife to die.

That night, after the rest of the family was asleep, Sri was on his knees. He knew the Jhakri's magic hadn't worked and yet he knew, deep in his heart that somewhere there was a God. Somewhere there had to be a God who had power, real power. So Sri called out into the darkness: "If there is any God, if there is a real God somewhere, make yourself known to me! What else will I do?"

But no answer came that night. Sri eventually crashed onto his bed and fell asleep, but on another night he had a dream. He saw a building in a town with a brightly coloured roof and someone spoke to him, "Take your wife there," the voice said, "the people there will pray for your wife and she will be healed."

The next day Sri was filled with a strange kind of hope. He looked down the hill towards the valley which held the closest road. All he had to do now was take his wife to that road, get on a bus and go looking for the brightly coloured roof. But getting Shanti-maya down to the road wasn't that easy. Nepal has a lot of villages perched on the tops of ridges, accessible only by foot up hundreds of steep stone steps. No ambulance would be coming to Sri's village any time soon. So Sri did what the Nepali village people do when they need to take someone to the hospital. He took a dokho basket, lined it with a blanket and then carefully placed his frail wife

in it. He told his children to be good and hefted the basket up onto his back then proceeded to carry Shanti-maya down the hill, step after step until they reached the road.

At the road they boarded an already crowded bus which drove towards the nearest town. As they were rounding the last bend before the houses started crowding each other Sri saw, out the window, a building that matched the one he had seen in his dream. "How do I get to that building?" he asked a woman who sat

near them. "Go through the main part of town, over a bridge, up past the small shrine and down the narrow road," she said. After the bus had stopped, Sri lifted his wife back up into the basket and started walking again.

Eventually they reached the building and Sri told the people there his story. He found out that they were Christians. "OK, let us pray for your wife," they said. Sri watched and listened very carefully as the men prayed over his dying wife, and he waited afterwards for something amazing to happen, but nothing did, not

straight away anyway... but by the time they had talked some more and drunk a cup of tea Shanti-maya's face looked a little brighter. By the time they reached the bus she was able to hold herself up in her seat. She still needed to be carried up the stone steps to their village but when she saw her children she was able to bend down and give them a hug.

Gradually, bit by bit, day by day, Sri watched his wife get better. Without the help of any medicine, or the charms from any Jhakri, she was growing stronger. Sri

knew that his cry on that dark night, to the true and real God, had been heard. His wife was getting better through the power of this living God.

One day, several months later, Sri took the walk down those steep steps again, but this time he wasn't carrying his wife. This time she was walking with him. They took the same bus, and followed the narrow road back to the building with the brightly coloured roof. They were going to ask some more questions. They wanted to know this God for themselves.

For he is the living God and he endures forever; his kingdom will not be destroyed, his dominion will never end. He rescues and he saves; he performs signs and wonders in the heavens and on the earth. Daniel 6:26 and 27

Never go Trekking Alone!

Whated is a building that sells medicine, but is not a pharmacy, has doctors, but is not a hospital, and arranges helicopter flights, but is not an airport?

It is a Himalayan rescue centre. But rescue from what? you might be asking. From the ferocious Yeti? Hungry snow leopards? No. Rescue from something more subtle and sneaky than that. Something that creeps up on you if you walk too fast. Something that makes your head hurt and makes you think crazy thoughts. It is almost as if the mountains themselves are making you sick. What am I talking about? Acute Mountain Sickness.

Colin and Terry were trekking buddies. Colin was a doctor, and Terry a teacher. Both were very fit and very keen. They had dreams of sledging on 'crazy carpets' near Everest Base Camp. Although they were both very strong men, Terry was the faster walker. Even with a full pack he would keep the lead while Colin trudged along happily behind. One day while they were making their way around the Annapurna mountain range, however, Colin suddenly got a burst of energy and began walking faster. He soon overtook Terry and the other members of the trekking group. He looked back over his shoulder at one stage and told the others that he would meet them further down hill at a local tea shop. Everyone else agreed and watched Colin march off into the distance. Later, when Terry's group reached the tea shop, they couldn't see Colin anywhere. They all assumed that he must have gone on ahead to the trekking lodge at Muktinath. So they drank their tea and then continued on as well.

But at Muktinath they didn't find Colin. They asked in all the lodges and hotels but no one had seen Colin or even heard of him. Terry began to get a bit concerned. Colin was more prone to mountain sickness than he was, maybe something had happened to him.

Mountain sickness is what happens to our bodies when we go too high too fast. Mountaineers and trekking guides recommend that you climb no faster than 300 meters each day and then rest to give your body time to adjust. The problem is that the higher you go the less oxygen is in the air and although we can get acclimatized to lower amounts of oxygen it does take time to do so. If you don't acclimatize gradually you can get ill. Headaches and nausea are the first symptoms. Breathlessness, even when resting, disorientation, confusion, the inability to walk in a straight line, all these things can happen to someone who has mountain sickness. If the person does not get help and start descending quickly their body begins to break down, and they can die.

Colin didn't die. He just got lost. Further back along the trail came another group of trekkers taking their time along the mountain paths. They were passing a ravine when someone noticed Colin wandering around at the bottom of it. He had taken a right turn instead of left and ended up confused and disorientated, not sure of how to get out of the ravine. He was feeling dizzy and sick and was sweating with fear. Someone called out to him and got his attention, then slowly and carefully directed Colin to a route by which he could climb out of the ravine. With his hands and knees scraping on the gravel he made his way back up the side, till he reached the top. Then he was escorted back down hill to Muktinath to rest and recover. Terry was sure glad to see Colin then.

The best thing to do to reduce the effects of mountain sickness is to go back down. Sometimes, however, mountain sickness can effect your thinking too. Terry told me a story of another trekker who got lost. When some people found him and explained to him that he needed to go down and visit the rescue centre, he smiled and nodded. The group started walking again, and after a while looked back to see how he was doing, but he was not there. He had smiled and nodded, and then turned in the opposite direction and walked into a farm yard! They headed back, forced him to turn around and made him march down to get help.

The Bible says that as Christians we are to *"Carry each other's burdens" (Galatians 6:2)* this doesn't mean that if you and I go trekking together you would carry my pack and I would carry yours. It means that we should help each other out, look out for each other. Sometimes life gets tough. Our friends might ask us to do things we know are not right, we get tempted to slack off, or we just get stuck in a rut of not knowing how to be who Jesus wants us to be. (Do you ever get to thinking things like "well Jesus never had to put up with my little brother!?") It is in times like this that we need Christian friends to help us. We don't want them to lecture us, although sometimes maybe they have to tell us what to do, but if they can just be there, and care, it is as if they are carrying our pack with us.

The Bible says *"Two are better than one, because they have a good return for their work: If one falls down, his friend can help him up. But pity the man who falls and has no one to help him up!" Ecclesiastes 4:9 and 10*

Note: Colin and Terry made it to Everest Base Camp in April 2004, but Colin got quite sick again. He has now decided that he has had enough. "I'm never going trekking again in my life!" he said.

Man-Eater!

When I was eight years old, and my two brothers were only five and three, my family came to Nepal for a holiday. I remember taking a long overnight bus ride to reach a hotel. I remember my dad throwing a bucket of water out the window in the middle of the night to try and frighten away the brawling cats. And I remember straining my ears to hear the footsteps of a tiger... .

At the Royal Chitwan National Park, one of Nepal's most famous nature reserves we stayed in a large tent-like bungalow. One morning we woke at dawn and climbed onto the back of an elephant. We then wobbled off into the parkland. "Look for tigers" our guide had told us from where he sat on the elephant's neck. So I looked. I was sure that I would see one, my brothers were too fidgety, they kept waiting to see the elephant pee again. My mum and dad were just relaxing

and enjoying the view, but I was really looking. I can even remember the dark mud on the jungle floor and the one tiger footprint the guide pointed out to us, but we didn't see a wild tiger.

Since then I have been able to visit various zoos and seen the massive Bengal tiger up close. I spotted my last tiger from the view point over the tiger cage at Kathmandu zoo. It was lying asleep in the shade of a man-made cave. The tigers that are native to this part of Asia are fascinating! They are so much bigger than you

think. You see them on TV and sure, they look large and frightening, but up close, when you are meters away from them, and you are watching them being fed in the cage in front of you, they are terrifying! That is when you remember that you are staring at a man-eater.

Tigers do not normally eat people. Most of their food is easily found within the borders of the nature reserves in which they live. Tigers usually hunt at night and unless they are looking for a mate, or guarding young cubs, they tend to travel alone. They commonly prey on the wild deer and antelope. There are many species of deer in this region so there is not normally a food shortage, but it is interesting to note that a tiger will eat anything it can kill. They have been known to hunt and eat wild boar, baby rhino and even sloth bears. In drought or difficult times when food does get scarce a tiger can catch fish, birds and even frogs to fill its stomach. Occasionally they will venture out of the jungle and into a local village farmyard to steal cattle. An average full grown male tiger can have a body length of over 2 metres and a shoulder height of 1 metre. It can weigh an enormous 200 kilograms!

Having all this readily available food and the tendency

to avoid human contact if possible, means that it is extremely unusual for tigers to attack people. Even when deliberately aggravated a tiger will usually growl a warning before attacking a person or deciding to retreat itself. There was a tiger in Chitwan, however, who had given up on most of his natural food and had begun to prey on the local people. One newspaper report I read claimed that the tiger had already been blamed for eight deaths and had just attacked a group of people on a picnic. One man at that picnic only survived by quickly climbing a tree and holding on. The tiger reportedly lay underneath the tree for a couple of hours, waiting for the man to come down, before it gave up and went away. Five other people in the group that day were not so lucky.

But what would turn one of these animals, with a large selection of meat available in the jungle each day, to venture into unfamiliar territory in search of human flesh? Apparently a man-eating tiger is not as strong as you would think. It is probably an old or injured tiger who is unable to catch regular prey. Aged, slow tigers soon discover that humans make an easy meal. They don't run as fast as deer and don't threaten to stab the tiger with their horns like a rhino might. Once the tiger gets the taste for human flesh it almost always loses interest in all other food. The local villages are no longer safe, and such a tiger needs to be destroyed.

A tiger with a record of killing and eating thirteen people is not the sort of tiger I want to face, even on the back of an elephant. I cannot look at a tiger without being taken back with awe. Awe at their size, their beauty, their strength. Although I have seen people get up close to these beasts, and I have even patted a very large baby one, I cannot think about tigers without remembering that they can be dangerous.

It is a bit like that with God. How can we think about God without remembering his Holiness? Our God is an Awesome God! The strength of a tiger is nothing compared to God's power. God's beauty is deeper than any appearance that we could ever see. Do you know the story of Moses when he spoke with God on Mount Sinai? (Exodus 34:29-30) Moses' face shone with such brilliance afterwards that he had to put a veil over it so as not to frighten the people of Israel. And yet, even with this beauty and power, God still gets angry. He is a righteous God, which means that he hates sin, he can't stand it. But just as the tiger growls softly before it acts, God also gives us a chance. The Bible says that God is "slow to anger and abounding in love". He offers us salvation and waits for us to grab a hold of it. Yes, our God is awesome, our God is powerful and mighty and holy, but he is also full of compassion and the grace to forgive. Sometimes there is nothing else to do but stand back and say "Wow!"

But you are a forgiving God, gracious and compassionate, slow to anger and abounding in love. Nehemiah 9:17

Great is the LORD and most worthy of praise; his greatness no one can fathom. Psalm 145:3

Elephant Thieves

When you think of elephants what do you think of? Huge, large-eared things trampling the savanna?

The elephants in the Himalayan region are actually Asian elephants and they are quite different than the elephants in Africa. The most easily recognizable feature is the size of their ears. The African elephant has much larger ears than the Asian. They both have tusks, but the

Asian ones are lighter and shorter. The Asian elephants also have a downward sloping backbone. But they are still big when you are up close to them and incredible to ride on. No wonder the ancient kings of this area rode on elephants, the view is terrific!

There are many national parks in Nepal, the largest being Chitwan National Park where the favourite recreation for tourists is looking for tigers on the backs of elephants, but further east, still on the Terai (the flat plain area that runs along the south of Nepal), I heard a story about wild elephants. Wild drunk elephants.

Don't believe me? It is true!

Can you imagine lying asleep in your mud-walled house with a straw thatch roof and feeling the floor shake a bit. You wake up. Earthquake! you think, but no. It is a thud, thud, thud, like someone big walking outside. Incredible Hulk! You think. Godzilla!

And then there is silence, then the rustle of straw and a deep sniffing sound and then a huge leathery trunk peeps itself under the corner of your roof and snakes its way into your house, sniffing, sniffing, sniffing... .

This is what has been happening in some parts of Nepal and North-East India. Elephants have become alcoholics.

They have charged into villages in search of roksi (the locally brewed alcohol) and literally smelt their way into people's homes. I heard one story of a home that now has a huge elephant footprint in the centre of its metal folding bed! They have broken shop windows, broken village gates, pulled the walls down of some houses all in their desperate search to quench their unnatural thirst.

Naturally the elephants live peacefully. Their homes are in the jungles and it would be only occasionally that they would 'trespass' onto cultivated fields and raid the corn or rice crops. But nowadays, as the human world desperately expands and the forests are cut into, the meetings between elephants and people can get violent. An elephant has been known to lift a man up by its trunk and fling him against a tree trunk in anger. And now some of these animals have acquired a taste for alcohol, increasing the tension even more. Any peaceful nature they used to have, where they roamed the fields and all the local people had to worry about was their crushing some rice occasionally, has gone. The elephants are fierce angry beasts.

Some villages now have a 'no alcohol' rule in order to keep the elephants away and keep their village standing upright. One village I was told about has even set up an electric fence, which worked for a while, until the elephants learnt how to cross it. The elephants now break branches from trees and lay them across the live wires, then carefully standing on the branch they cross the wire without being stung. They have become desperate and cunning in their search for roksi.

Hearing about these elephants reminds me of sin. Some sins can become addictive. We know it is wrong, but we still want to do it. There is only one cure for sin and that is Jesus. He is the only one who has the power to change us, right from inside and set us back on the track of being the amazing creatures he designed us to be. When we focus on him, and what he went through to enable us to be children of God, it makes it harder to sniff out and do the wrong thing. If we trust only ourselves when we try to do what is right, we are very likely to mess up. But with Jesus on our team, the battle against sin is a winning one, even if it is still a battle.

Let us throw off everything that hinders and the sin that so easily entangles, and let us run with perseverance the race marked out for us. Let us fix our eyes on Jesus, the author and perfecter of our faith... Consider him who endured such opposition from sinful men, so that you will not grow weary and lose heart. Hebrews 12: 1-3

Swept Away

Did you know that in the Nepali language there is no word for waterfall? The country is so mountainous that most rivers contain many waterfalls of various sizes, so there is, to a Nepali mind, no difference between the water than runs straight, or the water that tumbles down a cliff. They are both rivers and the Nepali word for river is 'khola'. There are hundreds of rivers in Nepal, most of them have their beginnings high up in the Himalayas and then they twist and travel through the hills, down to the plains. Some even join up to the famous Ganges River in India and make their way out into the sea.

In the dry months over winter (that is November to February) the Rivers are at their lowest, some seem to disappear altogether. But as the climate gets warmer and the ice on the mountains begins to melt the rivers start growing. Dry creek beds become trickles and when the tropical monsoon rains hit the hills, the rivers rise and swell, gathering speed and power. The strength in these rivers can break the base of a bridge and suck it away from the foundations. It leaves enormous concrete blocks stranded hundreds of metres down stream and queues of buses and trucks on its banks trying to find another way across the swollen stream. The rivers in Nepal are awesome, but dangerous.

One day in May, Rebekah's Sunday School (which actually meets on a Saturday because here people work on Sundays and go to church on Saturdays) went to the river for a picnic. They went to a place called Pame which is where a local river forks leaving two streams running parallel. It is a good place for a picnic because there is plenty of open space, some flat ground for playing games and some shallow water for paddling in.

They arrived early enough to prepare the picnic breakfast: vegetable curry, boiled eggs, flattened rice and tea. Rebekah and Mariam helped with the serving and washing up and then joined the others in some games. Afterwards the girls headed down to the shallow part of the stream to play.

None of the children on the picnic that day knew how to swim properly, but no one was really concerned because they were only paddling in the shallow waters. Rebekah and her friends stood in the knee deep water and splashed each other. They were being watched by one of the women from church called Cheeja and everyone was wet and laughing, until Rebekah's foot got stuck.

The ground at the bottom of the river where Rebekah had stood was soft and muddy and her left foot became bogged and stuck. At first she just laughed "My foot's stuck in the mud!" she giggled, wriggling her leg to free it. But as she wriggled the tugging set her off balance and she stumbled and fell face down in the water. If she had known how to swim that may have helped her, but she didn't know and as she panicked underwater the slight current of the stream pulled her foot loose and began to drag her down stream. As the water got suddenly deeper Rebekah tried to push herself out of the water, but her feet kept slipping and her flailing arms didn't know what to do, she sank back under water and blacked out.

From the river bank Cheeja had been anxiously watching Rebekah float away.

"Guhar! Guhar!" she called out to the other adults sitting up stream, "Help!" She ran along the bank following Rebekah's body, waiting anxiously, praying desperately that someone would know how to swim and pull the girl out.

One man finally jumped into the now deep and fast flowing river and dragged Rebekah out. Her skin had turned blue and she wasn't breathing. Cheeja, the other adults and all the children gathered around Rebekah. No one had any resuscitation skills, they only knew how to pray. And so they prayed hard, crying as they spoke, and somehow, it seems a miracle, Rebekah heard their voices and cries and opened her eyes.

Rebekah was saved, but about two weeks later, when

the rivers in Nepal had grown even more fierce, I saw a coffin being nailed shut outside the small house only doors away from where Rebekah lived. A coffin is a strange thing in Nepal, where most people are cremated, but this family were Christians. Who was in the box? A boy, the same age as Rebekah. He also had been swept away, but faster and more savagely. Days later someone pulled his body from the river, kilometres away from where he had played.

You know, being a Christian doesn't mean that bad things are not going to happen to you. The current we face each day may not be a huge river that pushes boulders down stream like pebbles, but we do go out each day into a world that has already decided it doesn't like what we believe. We haven't been guaranteed an easy ride, but God is still God. He still created the world. He still formed the mountains. He still holds the stars. We need to decide, before we step onto the river bank of life each day, whose hand are we going to hold onto and whose guidelines are worth listening to.

I have told you these things, so that in me you may have peace. In this world you will have trouble. But take heart! I have overcome the world. John 16:33

I'll be the Butterfly

What can I hold on the end of a stick which would make you run away? What flies like a kite in the wind when it is big but makes you scream when it is small? A Jusli-Kira.

A what?

A Jusli-Kira.

That is the Nepali word for what we would call a hairy caterpillar. Why would a caterpillar make you run away screaming? Because the caterpillars in Nepal are not very friendly. Recently I saw one that was over 10 centimetres long. It was lying on a stone wall and it looked just like a long fluffy dog which had its brown hair parted right down its back. I have seen smaller caterpillars with bright yellow sticky-uppy hair. I have seen big fat green ones which look like they are wearing black cycling helmets. I have seen ones that have bald heads and long flowing tails, and then ones that have multicoloured spiky hairdos near their faces. Whatever sort they are I don't like them. If you get the fur of one of these Jusli-Kira's on your skin it can sting like mad! A tiny rash could start to spread all over your body, the contact point may even turn into a large open sore. Some of these little critters can even squirt a sort of stinging poison at you if you are not careful. In Nepal we do not touch caterpillars.

Sometimes I think it is a shame. I would like to collect them and see what they will grow into. Nepal has some wonderful butterflies and moths, and some very clever ones. There is a certain type of butterfly that my children and I like to watch in our landlord's front garden. If it is a nice sunny day small grey-blue butterflies come to visit the flowers. If you don't look carefully at them you might get a bit confused as to which end is the head end. The butterfly has a bottom which looks like a face, in fact it actually looks more like a face than its actual face does! At the end of the butterfly's wings there are two long points which have eye-like markings on them. God gave this butterfly the ability to trick its predators into thinking it was looking in the other direction. Can you imagine another bug or lizard trying to make this butterfly its lunch and sneaking up on it only to find it was looking him straight in the eye the whole time?

There is another type of butterfly here that also amazes me and it too has a trick under its wing. It is the Orange Oakleaf butterfly. This butterfly has beautiful blue and orange markings on the top sides of its wings. Flying around it would very likely catch your attention and make you turn and look. But the very same butterfly can rest among the dead leaves of the jungle floor and you would be unable to see it. It is one of several types of butterfly in Nepal and the surrounding region that has a camouflage ability. The undersides of the Orange Oakleaf's wings have dull leaf-like markings. When it is sitting on the jungle floor with its wings folded shut it looks just like any of the leaves around it. Amazingly the leaf colour of its wings can change with the changing seasons, just like the leaves from the trees.

The Orange Oakleaf can remind us about how we are to act. Jesus said to his followers, *"You are the light of the world... let your light shine before men, that they may see your good deeds and praise your Father in heaven. Matthew 5: 14 and 16*

Like the butterfly with its wings spread open, showing the fantastic blue and orange, our love of Jesus should be obvious to those around us. But, what about the undersides of the butterfly's wings? They are dull and make it easy for the butterfly to hide and remain unseen, does this mean that we shine for Jesus only when we feel like it and then act just like everybody else when we don't?

I don't think so.

When Paul was writing about his ministry, which involved hundreds of people learning about Jesus and being taught the Scriptures, he said *"To the Jews I became like a Jew, to win the Jews. To those under the law I became like one under the law,... so as to win those under the law."* 1 *Corinthians 9: 20*

He tried to understand the way other people thought, how they felt and what they did, so that he knew how to best present Jesus to them.

Here in Nepal we make decisions everyday about what we wear, how we talk, whether we hold hands in public or not, because we do not want to offend people so much that they would reject Jesus because of what we do.

When Jesus asked us to shine, he also wanted us to think. Like the Orange Oakleaf we do two things at once. We shine for Jesus so other people can tell we have something special in our lives, but we also need to act with care for what others, who don't know Jesus yet, feel.

And may we, as people who say we love Jesus, never act in a way that makes people run and scream. Let's skip that hairy caterpillar stage, shall we?

I do all this for the sake of the gospel, that I may share in its blessings. 1 Corinthians 9: 23

Scars from a Leopard

The office was busy the day Tek Bahadur arrived from the village. "Jaimasih" he said lightly, his palms meeting at his chest in the local Christian greeting. "Jaimasih," the office staff replied without looking up. "How are you?" they asked.

"Oh, I'm fine," said Tek wondering when they would really begin to notice him. He had come in for some training. It had taken him a fair walk, a bus ride, another bus ride and another walk (dodging three buffaloes) to get here. He sat on one of the benches near the window and pulled his baseball cap down tighter shadowing the scars on his head.

Eventually the others put away their books and turned to face him. "How is life back in the village?" Jiwan asked him. "Oh, it's fine," said Tek shrugging.

"What about your mother and father, what do they think about you becoming a Christian?" Ramesh asked.

"Oh, they are fine," said Tek again.

"Oh come on, everything cannot be fine!" said Jiwan. He stood up and pushed Tek playfully. "What about your stomach?" he asked poking Tek in the gut. "Or your head? Any headaches?" he tipped Tek's hat off and then stood back startled. He and Ramesh stared at Tek's head, their mouths open in astonishment. Tek's head was covered with fresh scars. Jagged scars that ran in scraping lines across his face, down from his forehead and back into his hair.

"What has happened?" they asked together.

"A leopard," said Tek.

The scars on Tek's face were a few weeks old. There

had obviously been stitches, but they had been removed and the wounds were healing well enough, but the evidence of the leopard attack would be there to stay.

There were no gas ovens in Tek's village and on the day Tek had been attacked it was simply his turn to go and collect firewood from the nearby forest. He had been walking in the jungle between his village and another one looking for handy-sized pieces of timber that they could use for fuel. He had collected quite an amount and was stacking it into his dokha basket when he heard muffled footsteps behind him. At first he had thought it was one of his friends from the village, but when he turned around he was staring face to face with a fierce wild cat.

It is not that common to hear of leopard attacks. Naturally they are tree climbers, and can be more elusive than tigers. The local people have even said that the leopard can read minds because it is so hard to find. Occasionally leopards do attack people, but usually if they are intimidated or teased. I have heard of leopards coming into the outskirts of Pokhara and running away with someone's chickens or small dog, that is common enough, but not an apparently non-aggravated attack on a person. Tek was obviously alarmed. He put up his hands, one of them holding a piece of firewood in defence, but the leopard walked closer. Unlike Tek, it was not afraid. It jumped up on top of Tek, the weight of its body almost knocking him to the ground. Tek struggled with the animal, but it clawed at him angrily. Most of the leopard's blows came across Tek's face and head making the gashed scars that Jiwan and Ramesh now stared at horrified.

"So how did you escape?" gasped Ramesh, "surely you would have been eaten!"

"If he was eaten he wouldn't be here," said Jiwan. "It must have been a miracle."

Tek nodded. He knew he was the only Christian from his village. Although he had told his parents about his decision to follow the living God they had not come with him. They, and the rest of his village held firmly to Hindu beliefs and the daily rituals this involved. "God saved me," explained Tek simply as he replaced his cap. "He was there. I could feel His presence, somehow, while the leopard was trying to kill me. God wouldn't let it kill me. Our God was there the whole time."

Ramesh and Jiwan sat down stunned and shook their heads. It had been a miracle. How else would Tek have been able to fight off such a vicious attack?

"There is just one thing... " said Tek after a while, "I don't know why he saved me. He didn't have to. I would have gone to heaven if I had died. But I think God saved me for a reason. He has something he wants me to do, pray with me that I will know what His plan for my life might be."

Have you ever wondered what God wants you to do? There are many verses in the Bible that talk about God having a plan for his people. Jeremiah 29:11 says *"For I know the plans I have for you, declares the LORD."*

God knows why he wouldn't let the leopard destroy Tek's life. Perhaps Tek, being the only Christian from his area, will be used by God to tell others about Jesus. Perhaps Tek's scars will tell the story by themselves. Perhaps Tek will live each day in dependence on God and this will be a magnet to those who seek the truth. Perhaps we could say the same about you? God knows why you are who you are. He knows what you like and what you are good at, he knows the plan he has for your life too. When we read the Bible we come to know what

God is like and what he wants us to do. Just looking at the life of Jesus can tell us so much. So when you think about the future, or when your aunty asks you (again!) "what are you going to do when you grow up?" think about Tek and his scars and God's purpose for our lives.

And what does the LORD require of you? To act justly and to love mercy and to walk humbly with your God. Micah 6:8

Snake? No Thanks

About thirty years ago Ross and Kathleen came from New Zealand to Nepal. They came to live with the Chepang people. At that time there were no roads into Chepang land. The people group were very isolated. Not much was known about the Chepang, but Ross and Kathleen knew they wanted to work with them so they collected dried vegetables and food stuff, mattresses, cooking and basic medical supplies and packed all of this and their two boys, Philip and Martin, in baskets on porters' backs. Then they set off into the jungles and up worn Chepang paths until they reached the small village of Maiserang.

In Maiserang they were able to rent a small village house from one of the local families and they settled to live there for the time they would stay in the village. Their house was made in the traditional Chepang style. It was built from mud bricks and was split into two levels. The lower half had a fireplace in the centre of the room and had no windows. There was a thick notched wooden pole that acted as a ladder between the upstairs and downstairs. Up this pole was another room which was directly under the straw thatched roof. There was a window in this level, but it was only small, and the floors of both levels were covered with smooth orange mud, hammered down and hard.

Life in the village quickly fell into routine. Ross and Kathleen began to learn the Chepang language and make some friends. Sometimes Ross and his friends would head off into the surrounding jungles to go hunting or do some research. It was on one of these days, when Ross was overnighting in another village, that Kathleen had to be completely aware and alert because something had come to visit and she was going to have to deal with it.

The children had just finished their evening meal and it was bath time. Kathleen had set up the basin of warm water at the base of the notched pole and in it she had placed Philip, who was then five years old, to take a bath. He was playing happily away so Kathleen bundled Martin upstairs to where their mattresses lay, one next to the other, to put his pyjamas on. She lay him down and began taking off his nappy preparing herself to battle against his baby strength to make him lie still. But for once Martin wasn't wriggling. He wasn't looking at her either. He was staring at Philip's mattress bed.

" Mummy," he said calmly in his baby voice, "'dere is a 'nake on Pilip's bed."

Kathleen was lucky that she didn't poke the last pin right into Martin's tummy because he was right. There it was, curled up on the end of Philip's mattress keeping its eyes calmly focused on the half naked baby. A real live snake.

Kathleen didn't take the time to measure, photograph or identify that snake. She didn't think about how it was probably only lying there trying to keep warm from the cool outside air. She didn't even remember how frequently the villagers had chased snakes out of their own thatched roofs, she just picked up Martin and yelled down the pole to Philip.

"Get out of the bath!"

"But, I'm not finished... ."

"Get out!" Kathleen yelled. And Philip moved just in time. The sudden movement and noise from Kathleen had disturbed the snake from its rest and it had begun sliding towards the pole. "Hurry up Philip! Get out and move away!" Kathleen yelled. She swatted at the snake and it slid, then fell down the hole and right into the basin of water. Kathleen quickly climbed down the pole too and, after putting Martin and Philip safely to one side, she picked up the mallet that they used to keep the floor firm and flat. The snake started moving. It slid out of the basin and onto the floor and began moving towards the dark corners of the house. 'I'm not having any snakes in my house,' thought Kathleen. "Stand clear," she called to the boys. She lifted the mallet over her shoulder and then swung bringing it down on the snake, hard and fast.

There are a lot of different types of snake in Nepal. Small blind snakes, dangerous pit vipers, and even some pythons which have been measured to over 4 meters in length! Some of the snakes are poisonous, some of them aren't, but poisonous or not they both seem to make it into people's homes. Most of the time the snake is just looking for some place nice and warm to sleep. In Ross and Kathleen's village house they had come in attracted by the warmth of the fireplace, but no doubt spent days hiding among the thatching of the roof. Snakes are frequent visitors in village homes, but they have also been found in homes and buildings in the cities.

While they were in language school in Pokhara one of our friends, Maurice, found a snake in the bathroom. He had found it wound tightly around the drainpipe under the sink. The thing that made Maurice stand back in wonder was that he had just sent his two children in to clean the bathroom. They had been in there playing and tidying for quite a while but had never once actually seen the snake. It was as if God had blinded them to seeing it and kept that snake from going anywhere near the children.

Both Kathleen and Maurice faced the danger of a snake in unexpected places and yet in both situations, and so many more that I have heard of, God protected them. They didn't know the snake would be there, but God knew all the time. He knew exactly where the snake was, and he knew what they needed to remain safe.

The Bible says that *"The LORD himself goes before you and will be with you; he will never leave you nor forsake you. Do not be afraid; do not be discouraged." Deuteronomy 31:8*

Even when unexpected things happen in our lives and we are surprised and afraid, God never is. He always knows what is happening and even when it seems alarming, or makes us worry about what might happen next, He is always in control. We don't always know what is going to happen to us, but we do know that God knows, and we CAN trust in Him.

Glossary of Unusual Words:

Terai The name given to the strip of plains along the southern border of Nepal.

Roksi A Nepali home brewed alcohol.

Guhar The Nepali word for "Help!"

Jhakri Shaman, witch-doctor type person, who does 'magic' on behalf of a Hindu god, often involves sacrifices or other strange rituals.

Jaimasih This is the Christian version of Namaste the traditional Nepali greeting. 'Jai' means 'hail to' or 'praise be to' and 'Masih' is messiah. So Jaimasih means horray for Jesus!

A dokho A large cone-shaped basket that can be carried on your back.

Pokhara A large city in Nepal, west of the capital city Kathmandu. This is where we live.

Tea shop There are lots of 'tea shops' in Nepal. They are like small simple cafes that sell tea, biscuits, Coke etc. Nepali tea is usually hot, milky and sugary, sometimes spiced.

Kathmandu The capital city of Nepal.

Trekking Hiking in the mountains.

Muktinath A small village on the Annapurna Circuit trekking route, 3710 meters above sea level.

Quiz

1. What is the name of the best look-out site in Pokhara?
2. Where does the Psalmist say our help comes from?
3. What is the name of the people group who live 1000 metres above sea-level in the foothills of the Himalayas?
4. Dokhos are mainly used for carrying things – what else are they used for?
5. In times of trouble, the little chicks listened to the clucking of their mother to know when they were safe. As well as listening to our parents, what should we do?
6. What food does the Rhesus monkey eat in the wild?
7. What distinguishing mark does the Himalayan Black Bear have on its chest?
8. No one knows if the Yeti is really in the Himalayas or if it is just a legend. How do we know God is real?
9. How can you tell the size of a bear by its footprint?
10. Sri's wife, Shanti-maya, was dying – how did she get well again?
11. Why do people suffer from mountain sickness if they climb too fast up high mountains?
12. What does it mean to carry each other's burdens?
13. What size can an average full grown male tiger grow to?
14. What type of elephants do you find in the Himalayan region?
15. Can you remember the Nepali word for river?
16. The elephants caused a lot of trouble in the villages when they got 'drunk'. What is the one and only cure for sin in our lives?
17. What is a Jusli-Kira?
18. Why do you think God saved Tek from being killed by the leopard that attacked him?
19. What is an unwanted frequent visitor in the village homes in the Himalayas?
20. What can we do when unexpected things happen and we are afraid and worried?

Answers

1. Sarangkot Hill.

2. The Lord, the maker of heaven and earth. Psalm 121:1 & 2.

3. Chepang.

4. Temporary hen pens.

5. Listen to God, read his word and obey his commandments.

6. Fruit, insects and seeds.

7. White V shape.

8. We see his existence in creation, his working in people's lives and his love is shown to us in the Bible. He promised that if we are looking for him we will find him. Jeremiah 24:4.

9. Multiply it by 2.5.

10. Because Christians prayed to God for her.

11. Because there is less oxygen and you need to acclimatise gradually.

12. We should care for each other and watch out for one another, especially when we go through hard times or are tempted to do things that are not right.

13. Body length 2 metres by 1 metre shoulder height.

14. Asian.

15. Khola.

16. Jesus - he is the only one who has the power to change us from inside when we ask him to forgive our sins.

17. A hairy caterpillar.

18. Because God had a purpose for his life and wanted him to tell others about Jesus.

19. Snakes.

20. We can trust God because he knows what is happening and he is always in control.

References:

Personal Interviews / email correspondence:
        Rebekah Tamang; Anne Herr; Ross and Kathleen Caughley; Morna Lincoln; Terry Lachance

Books:
Mishra, Hemanta R, and Mierow, Dorothy.
Wild Animals of Nepal. Ratna Pustak Bhandar, Nepal. 1976.
Majupuria. Trilock Chandra. Wild Is Beautiful. Introduction to the magnificent, rich and varied Fauna and wildlife of Nepal. S. Devi, India. 1981.
Finlay, H, Everist, R and Wheeler, T. Nepal. Lonely Planet Publications. Australia. 1999.
Whalley, P. Eyewitness Guides: Butterfly and Moth. Dorling Kindersley, London, 1988.
Periodicals:
National Geographic Magazine May 2003 "Everest" Pages 2-34.
Other resources:
"Mountains Sickness and other Hazards in the Nepal Himalaya" Brochure distributed by The Himalayan Rescue Association Nepal, PO Box 4944, Dhobichour, Lazimpat Kathmandu, NEPAL.

Penny Reeve was born in Australia and is with International Nepal Fellowship, supporting health and communitiy development work amongst the people of Nepal.

Staying Faithful - Reaching Out!

Christian Focus Publications publishes books for adults and children under its three main imprints: Christian Focus, Mentor and Christian Heritage. Our books reflect that God's word is reliable and Jesus is the way to know him, and live for ever with him.

Our children's publication list includes a Sunday school curriculum that covers pre-school to early teens; puzzle and activity books. We also publish personal and family devotional titles, biographies and inspirational stories that children will love.

If you are looking for quality Bible teaching for children then we have an excellent range of Bible story and age specific theological books.

From pre-school to teenage fiction, we have it covered!

**Find us at our web page:
www.christianfocus.com**